Teaching Tool

For William Shakespeare's Romeo and Juliet

Copyright © M.E. Richards (2021)

All Rights Reserved

Publisher: Scribblers' Ink

Cover, Map and Interior Design: C.C. Richards

Table of Contents

Introduction

Teaching a work that feels so familiar, but which is riddled with popular culture misconceptions, is a particular challenge. *Romeo and Juliet* is often a student's first exposure to Shakespeare; many of my students started this unit by declaring, "I hate Shakespeare!" Happily, because of the swords and the poison, they change their minds. The language scares them at first, but we read each line out loud and I explain meaning as we go. In no time, frequent explanations are not necessary. Clearly, what you need to start is the original text. In conjunction with the text, this Teaching Tool will provide a complete study. Here are some suggestions for the classroom time that have worked:

- Dramatic Readings: Students should read every word out loud; dramas need to be heard. Shakespeare needs to be heard! Roles can rotate regardless of gender or speaking fluency. Rearranging desks into a circle helps.
- Exposure to the Language of Poetry is paramount, specifically: Rhyme, Alliteration, Anaphora, Metaphor, Simile, Hyperbole, Paradox, Oxymoron, Onomatopoeia, Personification, Parallel Structure,
- Exposure to Language that builds levels of Meaning is crucial, specifically: Verbal and Dramatic and Situational Irony, Satire, Symbolism, Analogy, Allusion
- Each student should have a notebook specifically for this English class. The notebook is for taking notes from lectures (I put an outline on the board), defining any essential words, drawing a map to connect the work geographically (a map is included here for the teacher's benefit), character descriptions to recognize each individual voice, any research assigned, and for notes on the sequence of events in the play. A couple sentences on every scene will help with sequence order, understanding, and memory.
  - Collect the notebook at the end of the Study Unit for a homework/classwork grade.
- If something more is wanted, these are recommended for either your further enrichment or students' diversion:
  - *Barron's Simply Shakespeare, Romeo and Juliet*
  - Rudolph Academy's Crossword puzzles
  - Movie: Zeffirelli's *Romeo and Juliet*
  - *Painless Poetry*, by Mary Elizabeth

Introductory Lecture Outline for Shakespeare's *Romeo and Juliet* (20 min)

- Shakespeare's **political messages** in *Romeo and Juliet*:
    - Written between 1591-6 during the reign of Queen Elizabeth I, a Protestant.
    - Before Queen Elizabeth, Queen Mary I, a strict Roman Catholic, ruled;
        - Their father, King Henry VIII, had been a Roman Catholic but changed
            - He wanted to divorce Catherine of Aragon, allied with Spain, so he could marry Anne Boleyn
            - The Pope refused, primarily to not anger Spain
            - By creating the Church of England, King Henry polarized his people, pitting Protestants against Catholics
    - Shakespeare was Roman Catholic
    - Some Roman Catholics in England tried to sabotage the Protestant government of Queen Elizabeth.
    - Queen Elizabeth retaliated by hunting down Catholic spies, often priests from Rome.
    - The country's division is dramatized in *Romeo and Juliet* by the two leading families feuding, even though they are 'alike in dignity'
- Shakespeare's settings (place) are elsewhere so he cannot be accused of treason.
    - Italy was a favorite alternate location, though he had never traveled outside England.
    - No matter the setting, Shakespeare is always talking about England.
- *Romeo and Juliet* is one of Shakespeare's first tragedies
    - He showcases a flair for mixing tragedy with comedy and romance.
- **The Setting:** In the 1300 to 1400s, medieval Italy was composed of city states.
    - Each city state was independent; there was no central alliance.
    - Each city state had its ruler, usually a duke or a prince; Verona had a prince.
    - Each city state would have a few important, upper-class, privileged families.
        - These few families, along with the ruler and church, controlled the wealth.
        - The rest of the people were commoners, laborers.
    - **Act I - Verona** in the **summer,** it is very hot, the heat ignites tempers.
- Shakespeare's settings (time) are earlier so he can dramatize through contrast.
    - In 1590 England the average age of marriage was between 24 and 27;
        - 1400 Italy the girl would be 16 and the boy in his 20s.

- Marriage in medieval times was NOT a matter of love.
  - Girls were ruled by their fathers.
  - A girl's value was increased by her beauty and accomplishments, but her family's social and financial position were paramount.
  - Girls were kept secluded, within family circles, until marriage age
    - Marriage age for a commoner was around 16 (girl) and 20 (boy)
    - Marriage age for upper class could be as young as 12 (girl) or just at the point of puberty; widely variable for the boy.
    - Often the upper-class girl was introduced into society through parties, often masques, given by or for other upper-class families.
      - This way she could be shown to the right sort of young men and their families.
  - The upper-class girl's father looked for two attributes for his daughter's husband:
    - Wealth – of money and property - adds to father's economic status.
    - Connections – alliances with other powerful families adds to the father's influence: social and political power.
    - Husbands were found while the girls were quite young to guarantee:
      - She had not formed an earlier, unacceptable love interest,
      - She was still a virgin,
      - Obedience to her father would transfer seamlessly to her husband.
  - Upper-class boys might have traveled a bit, 'sowed their wild oats', before returning to their home city to find a bride.
  - The upper-class young man has more say in whom he marries; he looks for:
    - A good dowry if he has spent a significant part of his inheritance while traveling,
    - Otherwise, he looks for respectable connections, beauty, accomplishments, and a malleable, sweet manner.
- Juliet's father should have been looking to Romeo's family for a match, because:
  - They are "alike in dignity", or on the same high social level, prominent but not aristocracy.
  - Each has one child, if these children married their families would join and their wealth and influence would be doubled.
  - The only better match would have been with the Prince's family, aristocracy.

MAP OF ITALY DURING THE MIDDLE AGES
SWITZERLAND
M. OF MONTFERRAT
Milan
REP. OF VENICE
Verona
Venice
OTTOMAN EMPIRE
D. OF SAVOY
ASTI
D. OF MILAN
MANTUA
FERRARA
M. OF SALUZZO
D. OF MODENA
Ravenna
REP. OF FLORENCE
Florence
M. OF MONTFERRAT
REP. OF GENOA
REP. OF SIENA
PAPAL STATE
ADRIATIC SEA
Rome
Naples
KINGDOM OF NAPLES
Sardinia (SPAIN)
TYRRHENIAN SEA
IONIAN SEA
MEDITERRANEAN SEA
KINGDOM OF SICILY
Legend
= REP. OF VENICE
D. = Duchy
M. = Marquisate
Rep. = Republic
Distance between Verona and Mantua = 43.8 km

Medieval Walled City State

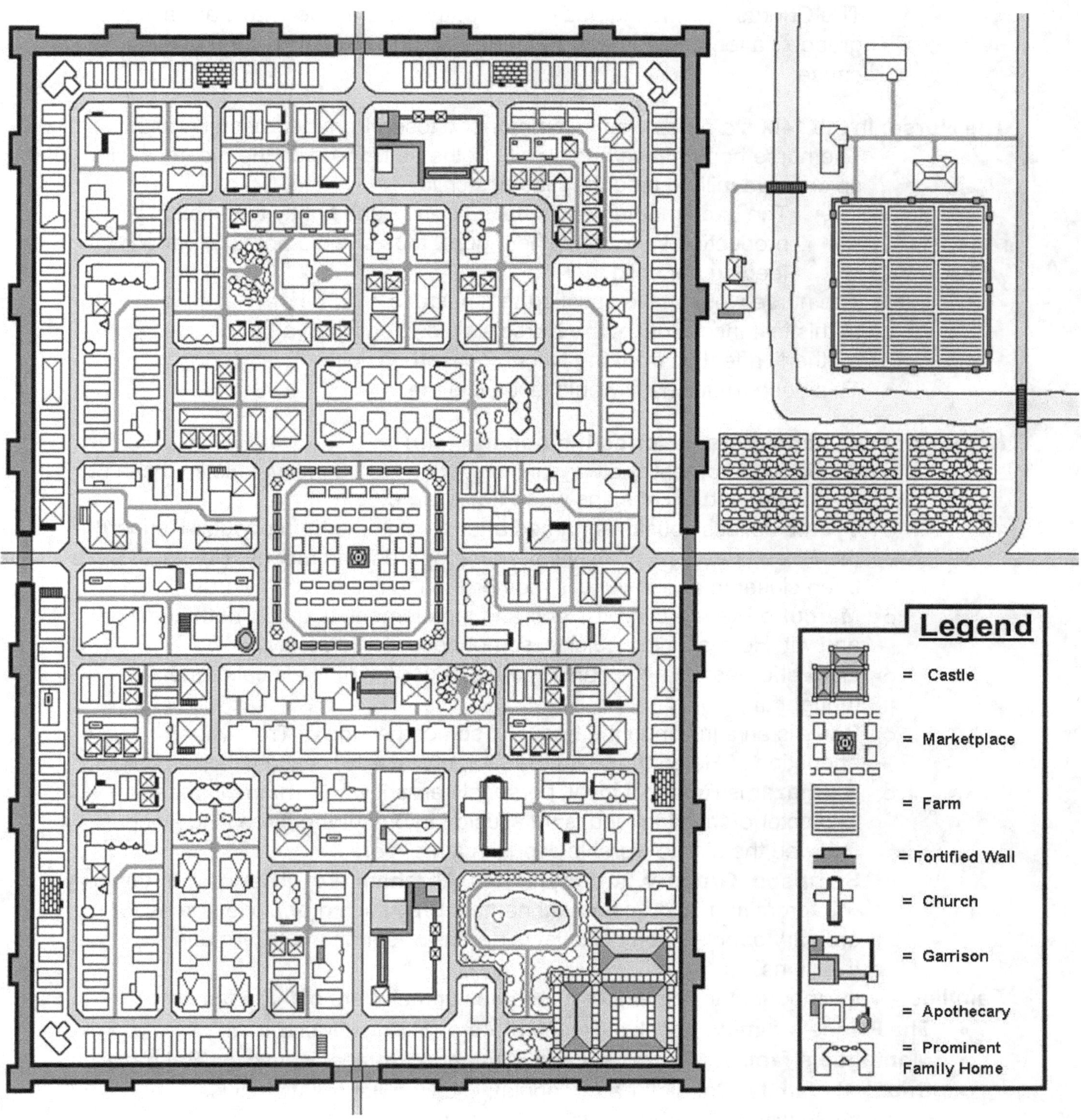

Lecture before Act 1   5 minutes

The Sonnet: This fourteen-line poem is the Prologue as it introduces **Act 1**
- Spoken by the Chorus, it is a story the audience probably would have known for Shakespeare borrowed the basic plot from multiple sources.
- The Chorus informs the audience that the two families have an "ancient grudge", a feud going back so far that no one remembers the original cause.

The Nurse: In the 1400s a nurse was a commoner chosen from her master's estate.
- The nurse had to have had a child at the same time as the master's wife, so she had milk to feed the master's child.
  - The Lady mother would have been bound tightly to inhibit milk production so to retain her figure, thus she did not take part in feeding her child.
- The nurse would have satisfied the master's child before her own.
- In this instance, Susan, the Nurse's child, died when a babe so all motherly affection from the Nurse focused on Juliet.
- This bond traditionally would last a lifetime.

Names of male characters describe their characters:
- **Romeo** is a romantic, always in love, wants to be in love; his love can be inconstant and full of sighs when not returned.
- **Tybalt,** Juliet's cousin, is named after a cat in the then popular Reynard the Fox stories – he is a sly cat, hot-tempered and moody. He would have been closer in age to Juliet's mother than to Juliet.
- **Mercutio** like mercury, the god and the element, is quick, both in action and wit. He reacts too quickly, so not necessarily wisely.
- **Benvolio** has what his name means, a good will. He is calm and thoughtful.
- **Paris** is an allusion to the beautiful son of the king of Troy whose abduction of Helen triggered the Trojan War – two nations 'alike in dignity'.
- **Balthazar** is Romeo's loyal, personal servant whose name is means 'protector of the king' and is an allusion to one of the three kings who followed the star to worship Jesus in a manger.
- **Sampson, Gregory, Antony, Peter, Abraham** are all servants in this play with prominent Old Testament names. Why such grandiose names for ordinary people? Irony? Reflects parental aspirations? Religious traditions?

Families – very important to remember the names of members of three families:
- **The Prince's family**: Escalus, Prince of Verona; Paris; Mercutio
- **Montague's family**: Montague; Lady Montague; Romeo; Benvolio; (Balthazar)
- **Capulet's family**: Capulet; Lady Capulet; Old Capulet (relative of Capulet not to be confused with Capulet), Juliet; Tybalt, (Nurse)

The Shakespearean Sonnet – a Poetry Writing Assignment (*due in one week*)

Write a sonnet on something about which you find deeply emotional, either with joy or sorrow (a friend, the polluted ocean? a death? bullies? A new baby sister?). Your sonnet could tell a story or describe a feeling that increases in complexity and intensity.

Your Sonnet must follow these **guidelines**:

1. The **Theme** of the Sonnet is **powerful and passionate**. In *Romeo and Juliet*, the first sonnet speaks of a hatred that has caused two families to fight for generations.

2. **Shakespearean Sonnets have a specific structure:**
   - 14 lines: 3 quatrains (4-line stanza) and one couplet (2-line stanza)
   - A strict rhyme scheme: abab; cdcd; efef; gg
   - The rhythm is iambic pentameter: 5 two-syllable units (feet), so 10 syllables per line
     - Each foot has an unstressed/stressed beat; like that found in 'de**sire**' or 'to **meet**'

3. **Sonnets develop their themes following this format:**
   - The first quatrain introduces the theme and situation;
   - The second quatrain develops the theme, introduces complications;
   - The third quatrain expresses the climax of the theme, the pinnacle;
   - The couplet offers the conclusion, solution.

The Sonnet can be written as one stanza of 14 lines or as **four stanzas: 3 quatrains** and a **couplet.** For examples of one stanza sonnets look at the Prologues of Acts 1 and 2 of *Romeo and Juliet.*

Assessment Rubric

Theme is powerful	/20
Voice is passionate	/20
Poem is **14 lines**	/5
Lines have **ten syllables** each	/10
(extra credit if iambic pentameter)	
Meaning/Story moves forward by quatrains	/15
Meaning/Story **concludes** in final couplet	/5
Rhyme scheme is followed strictly	/15
(rhymes are natural, not forced)	
Poem includes **Metaphor or Simile**	/5
Poem includes **Alliteration or Anaphora**	/5
Total	**/100**

Lecture before Act 2   **4 minutes**

- **Prologue – The Second Sonnet**
    - The purpose of this sonnet is to foreshadow Act 2 = Romeo's love for Juliet has a chance because it is returned.
    - Their families' enmity only inspires caution, not hatred in them.

- **The Ball** – from **Act 1** determines the trajectory of **Act 2**
    - It should have sealed the deal for Paris – a better match socially.
        - A match side-swiped by a less conventional, less polite approach
    - Opens the way for the balcony scene, which is so romantic and flirtatious it seals the deal for Romeo.
    - Opens the door to more personal violence since the ball is where Tybalt recognizes Romeo, his family's enemy, his home's intruder.
    - Extends Tybalt's excuse to continue the Capulet-Montague feud
        - Romeo's home intrusion/territorial violation overrides the Prince's orders

- **Friar Lawrence** – is introduced.
    - Represents the church and what is holy in God's eyes.
    - Is a herbalist, which is important later.
    - Is confessor or counselor and friend to Romeo, though certainly is also known to Juliet.
    - Is the one adult Romeo trusts to share his thoughts

Rationale for Quiz Type

The style of these quizzes overwhelms students at first, especially students who are used to skimming works of literature. Skimming leads to a foggy quagmire of not understanding. To pass these quizzes, students need to pay attention in class as they try to hear the voice of each character. Each quotation chosen clearly connects to the targeted character's voice.

Being able to identify the Act (Quiz#1) or Scene (Quizzes #2, #3) of each quotation shows an understanding of the sequence of events, the plot.

I strongly recommend the teacher allows students at this level to use their notebooks during quizzes. This ensures the notebooks are useful on more than one level, which may convince students to do an exceptional job. As well, knowing that the notebook is accessible for reference reduces stress.

Quiz #1 on Acts 1 and 2 of *Romeo and Juliet*

Name ____ Date _______________________________

I. Understanding Character

Here is a list of the major characters we have seen so far. If you understand the character, you will know his language style, his attitudes, his priorities, all of which are revealed in his speech.

Romeo	*Juliet*	*Chorus*
Montague	*Capulet*	*Prince Escalus*
Lady Montague	*Lady Capulet*	*Paris*
Benvolio	*Nurse*	*Mercutio*
Friar Lawrence	*Tybalt*	

Who said it?

Write the name of the speaker beside the excerpt, and then identify its Act:

1. ______________________________ 'Tis but thy name that is my enemy,
   Thou art thyself, though not a Montegue.
   What's Montague? It is nor hand, nor foot,
   Act ____________

2. ______________________________ I do but keep the peace. Put up they sword,
   Or manage it to part these men with me.
   Act ____________

3. ______________________________ Rebellious subjects, enemies to peace,
   Profaners of this neighbor-stainéd steel –
   Will they not hear? – What ho! You men, you beasts,
   Act ____________

4. ______________________________ This is the matter: - Nurse, give leave awhile,
   We must talk in secret. – Nurse, come back again.
   I have remembered me, thou's hear our counsel.
   Act ____________

5. ______________________________ He shall be endured.
   What, goodman boy? I say he shall. Go to.
   Am I the master here or you? Go to.
   Act ____________

6. ______________________________ What, drawn and talk of peace? I hate the word
   As I hate hell, all Montagues, and thee.
   Act ____________

7. _______________________   O, then I see Queen Mab hath been with you.
She is the fairies' midwife, and she comes
In shape no bigger than an agate stone
Act _______________

8. _______________________   O then, dear saint, let lips do what hands do.
They pray: grant thou, lest faith turn to despair.
…
Then move not while my prayer's effect I take.
Act _______________

9. _______________________   Now old desire doth in his deathbed lie,
And young affection gapes to be his heir.
That fair for which love groaned for and would die,
With Juliet matched, is now not fair.
*Act*_______________

10. _______________________   Of honorable reckoning are you both,
And pity 'tis you lived at odds so long.
But now, my lord, what say you to my suit?
…
Younger than she are happy mothers made.
*Act*_______________

11. _______________________   Holy Saint Francis, what a change is here!
Is Rasaline, that thou didst love so dear,
So soon forsaken? Young men's love then lies
Not truly in their hearts, but in their eyes.
*Act*_______________

12._______________________   O, where is Romeo? Saw you him today?
Right glad I am he was not at this fray.
*Act*_______________

II. Setting and Structures

The tale takes place in the city-state of _______________________.

It centers on an ongoing _______________________ between two prominent families.

The Chorus foreshadows the events and follows the poetic structure of the

_______________________, which is a poem with _______________________ lines.

Act 1 has _______________ scenes, while Act 2 has _______________scenes.

Name _______________________________________   Date ___________________________

I. Understanding Character

Who said it?

Write the name of the speaker beside the excerpt, and then identify its Act:

1. _______Juliet_______________   'Tis but thy name that is my enemy,
   Act _______2_______

2. _______Benvolio___________   I do but keep the peace. Put up they sword,
   Act _______1_______

3. _______Prince Escalus_______   Rebellious subjects, enemies to peace,
   Act _______1_______

4. _______Lady Capulet_________   This is the matter: - Nurse, give leave awhile,
   Act _______1_______

5. _______Capulet_____________   He shall be endured.
   Act _______1_______

6. _______Tybalt______________   What, drawn and talk of peace? I hate the word
   Act _______1_______

7. _______Mercutio____________   O, then I see Queen Mab hath been with you.
   Act _______1_______

8. _______Romeo______________   O then, dear saint, let lips do what hands do.
   Act _______1_______

9. _______Chorus______________   Now old desire doth in his deathbed lie,
   Act _______2_______

10. _______Paris_______________   Of honorable reckoning are you both,…
    Younger than she are happy mothers made.
    Act _______1_______

11. _______Friar Lawrence_______   Holy Saint Francis, what a change is here!
    Act _______2_______

12. _______Lady Montague_______   O, where is Romeo? Saw you him today?
    Act _______1_______

II. Setting and Structures

The tale takes place in the city-state of __Verona__. It centers on an ongoing

__feud__ between two prominent families. The Chorus foreshadows the events and

follows the poetic structure of the __sonnet__, which is a poem with __fourteen__ lines.

Act 1 has __five__ scenes, while Act 2 has __six__ scenes.

- **Perspective:**
  In less than two days, Romeo has met, flirted with, and married Juliet!

- **Structure of the Day:**
  - Morning heat, unrelieved from the day before, brings on out-of-control tempers – Scene 1
  - Afternoon heat brings the consequences of hot tempers to light and scrutiny
  - Evening's cool shadow allows for soft sweet private whisperings

- **What is Legal:**
  - The Prince rules all in civil matters – Escalus is the determiner of law, of punishment, even of life and death.
    - Prince Escalus has determined the feud is illegal
    - Two of his kinsmen, Mercutio and Count Paris, are getting entangled
  - Friar Lawrence rules, as the representative of the Church, in Spiritual matters
  - Man rules Woman – Lord Capulet legally rules Lady Capulet
  - Parent rules Child – Legally Lord Capulet rules Juliet; in his absence, Lady Capulet rules.

- **Wordplay:**
  - Oxymorons – emphasize the couple's contradictory situation: 'beloved enemy'
  - In Scene 1 and throughout the play, jests with the multiple meanings of Man: adult male, male servant, manhood
  - In Scene 2, Juliet makes puns with the homophones eye, I, ay

Quiz #2 on Act 3 of *Romeo and Juliet*

Name ____ Date ____________________________

I. Understanding Sequence – the order of things

Who said it?

Write the name of the **speaker** beside the excerpt, and then identify its **Scene**.

Montague	*Romeo*	*Lady Capulet*	*Nurse*	*Prince*
Escalus	*Tybalt*	*Capulet*	*Juliet*	*Paris*
Friar Lawrence	*Benvolio*	*Mercutio*		

1. ________________________ What, rouse thee, man! Thy Juliet is alive,
For whose dear sake thou wast but lately dead:
There art thou happy. Tybalt would kill thee,
But thou slowest Tybalt: there art thou happy
Scene _____

2. ________________________ I am hurt.
A plague o' both houses! I am sped.
Is he gone and hath nothing?
Scene ______

3. ________________________ What storm is this that blows so contrary?
Is Romeo slaughtered and is Tybalt dead?
My dearest cousin and my dearer lord?
Scene ______

4. ________________________ Hie to your chamber. I'll find Romeo
To comfort you. I wot well where he is.
Scene ______

5. ________________________ Sir Paris, I will make a desperate tender
Of my child's love. I think she will be ruled
In all respects by me.
Scene ______

6. ________________________ It was the lark, the herald of the morn,
No nightingale. Look, love, what envious streaks
Do lace the severing clouds in yonder east…
I must be gone and live, or stay and die.
Scene ______

7. ________________________ Ay, sir, but she will none, she gives you thanks.
I would the fool were married to her grave.
Scene ______

15

What aspect of the **Setting** plays a definite role in the climax of Act III?

____

Lady Capulet grieves for ___________________________; Lady Montague grieves for
___________________; The Prince grieves for _________________________.
What Laws stop Juliet from marrying Paris:
____ and

____.

Name ____ Date ____________________

I. Understanding Sequence – the order of things

Who said it?
Write the **name** of the speaker beside the excerpt, and then identify its **Scene**.

1. ____Friar Lawrence____   What, rouse thee, man! Thy Juliet is alive,
     Scene __3__

2. ____Mercutio____   I am hurt.
A plague o' both houses! I am sped.
     Scene __1__

3. ____Juliet____   What storm is this that blows so contrary?
Is Romeo slaughtered and is Tybalt dead?
     Scene __2__

4. ____Nurse____   Hie to your chamber. I'll find Romeo
     Scene __2__

5. ____Capulet____   Sir Paris, I will make a desperate tender
Of my child's love.
     Scene __4__

6. ____Romeo____   It was the lark, the herald of the morn,
     Scene __5__

7. ____Lady Capulet____   Ay, sir, but she will none, she gives you thanks.
     Scene __5__

What aspect of the **Setting** plays a definite role in the climax of Act III?
____the weather – the heat____

Lady Capulet grieves for _Tybalt_; Lady Montague grieves for __Romeo__; The
Prince grieves for __Mercutio__. What Laws stop Juliet from marrying Paris:
__Church Law-marriage is forever; Christianity has condemned bigamy since 285AD__;
__Verona's Civil Law against bigamy__ and __Parental Law – the father rules his child__.

Lecture before Act 4   **3 or 4 minutes**

- **Paris: wealthy kinsman of the Prince**
  - Chooses Juliet
  - Has her father's, Capulet's, approval
    - Would allow Capulet's family to rise in society
  - **Juliet** between a rock and a hard place
    - Has intentionally acted without consulting her father, to whom she owes allegiance and obedience
    - Has consulted her Nurse, an indulgent mother figure but without power
  - **Romeo** is satisfied with his decision because he:
    - Has consulted Friar Lawrence, a father figure with the power of Church authority
    - Has received permission and compliance from this father figure
  - **Role of Religion/Church**
    - Has authority alongside the Prince
    - Enforces Church Laws and Traditions
      - Church Law states that if the bride and groom are under 21, they need parental consent
      - Church law states that the marriage must be performed before two witnesses
      - Church law states that if a marriage has been performed but…
        - If consummation has not happened, the marriage can be declared null and void: annulled
        - if consummation has happened, the marriage is valid in God's eyes – cannot be annulled
      - Social laws dictate that only the Prince can override the authority of the father,
        - but not the authority of the Church

- **Friar Lawrence: a complex and conflicted character:**
  - As the Church's representative, has access to the Prince and Capulet
  - Acted with full knowledge of the State and Church laws
  - Acted as an indulgent father to Romeo but not a citizen compliant with State law
  - Wanted an end to the feud and viewed this Montague/Capulet alliance as a gift from God
  - Knows the feud is a secular issue, not a religious conflict, so is more under the authority of the Prince
    - Thus Friar Lawrence acts outside his authority knowingly
    - This knowledge explains his increasingly perilous risks

Quiz #3 on Act 4 of *Romeo and Juliet*

Name ____ Date ____________________

I. Understanding Sequence – the order of things

If you understand the character, you will know his speech, and you will know what characteristic triggers the events. *So,* **Who said it?** Write the **name** of the speaker beside the excerpt, and then identify its **Scene**:

Montague	*Romeo*	*Lady Capulet*	*Nurse*	*Prince*
Escalus	*Tybalt*	*Capulet*	*Juliet*	*Paris*
Friar Lawrence	*Benvolio*	*Mercutio*		

1. ______________________________

Go waken Juliet. Go and trim her up.
I'll go and chat with Paris. Hie, make haste,
Make haste. The bridegroom he is come already.
Make haste, I say.
Scene __________

2. ______________________________

Take thou this vial, being then in bed,
And this distilling liquor drink thou off;
When presently through all thy veins shall run
A cold and drowsy humor;
Scene __________

3. ______________________________

What , dressed and in your clothes and down again?
I must needs wake you. Lady, lady, lady! –
Alas, alas! Help, help! My lady's dead. –
Scene __________

4. ______________________________

Where I have learned me to repent the sin
Of disobedient opposition
To you and your behests, and am enjoined
By holy Lawrence to fall prostrate here
To beg your pardon. Pardon, I beseech you.
Scene __________

5. ______________________________

God shield I should disturb devotion! –
Juliet, on Thursday early will I rouse you.
Till then, adieu, and keep this holy kiss.
Scene __________

6. _______________________   Accursed, unhappy, wretched, hateful day!...
But one, poor one, one poor and loving child,
But one thing to rejoice and solace in,
And cruel death hath catch'd it from my sight!
*Scene*____________

7. Juliet has fears about taking the potion. Mention two of her fears:

____

____

Name ____ Date ___________________________

I. Understanding Sequence – the order of things

If you understand the character, you will know his speech, and you will know what characteristic triggers the events. *So,* **Who said it?** Write the **name** of the speaker beside the excerpt, and then identify its **Scene:**

1. ____Capulet____________ 	Go waken Juliet. Go and trim her up.
   Scene __4__

2. ____Friar Lawrence________ 	Take thou this vial, being then in bed,
   Scene __1__

3. ______Nurse____________ 	What , dressed and in your clothes and down again?
   I must needs wake you. Lady, lady, lady! –
   Scene __5__

4. ______Juliet____________ 	Where I have learned me to repent the sin
   Of disobedient opposition
   Scene __2__

5. ______Paris____________ 	God shield I should disturb devotion! –
   Juliet, on Thursday early will I rouse you.
   Scene __1__

6. ____Lady Capulet________ 	Accursed, unhappy, wretched, hateful day!...
   But one, poor one, one poor and loving child
   Scene __5__

7. Juliet has fears about taking the potion. Mention two of her fears:
   1. Dying from the poison because Friar Lawrence wants her dead so he will not be dishonored; 2. Being stifled in the vault by the horrific fumes so strangling before Romeo comes; 3. The spirits and festering shrouds will drive her mad; 4. The potion not working and she wakes up having to marry Paris

Romeo and Juliet: **The Oral Presentation** ....due in two weeks

Choose an excerpt of at least ten lines to present to the class. It must include a complete thought (do not stop mid idea).

- It must be memorized.
- You may do it with someone (creating an interactive scene) or on your own (a monologue); however, each speaker must have at least 10 lines. No more than two actors per presentation.

Before you recite your lines:

- present the context (Act, Scene and where in the plot sequence it comes);
- comment on its literary devices;
- comment on its significance to the play as a whole.

On the Day of your Presentation:

- You may come in costume.
- You may bring a prop.
- You may ask someone to be your prompter.

Before your Presentation **Turn in:**

- a written transcript, at least an outline.
    - Include the excerpt memorized,
    - the literary devices named and underlined,
    - and bullet points of the significance.

Romeo and Juliet—Oral Assessment Rubric

	Criterion A: Quality of Ideas		Criterion B: Presentation		Criterion C: Language
	How well does the speaker know and understand the subject matter? To what extent are the speaker's ideas relevant and focused? Is there evidence of critical thinking? Is there appreciation of language and style? Are ideas supported by relevant examples and illustrations?		How effective is the organization of the oral task? How coherent is the structure? Are examples and illustrations well integrated into the oral task?		How effective is the organization of the oral task? How coherent is the structure? Are examples and illustrations well integrated into the oral task?
0	Level 1 is not achieved	0	Level 1 is not achieved	0	Level 1 is not achieved
1-2	**The speaker has little awareness of the subject matter;** ideas are frequently irrelevant and/or repetitive; there is little analysis of the subject matter; little awareness of language and style is shown; ideas are not supported by examples and illustrations.	1-2	**Little organization is apparent;** the oral task has little structure; supporting examples and illustrations are not integrated into the oral task.	1-2	**The language lacks fluency and appropriateness;** there are many basic errors in grammar and sentence construction; there is little sense of register and style; there is little variety in vocabulary and idiom; frequent hesitations impede the flow of the exchange.
3-4	**The speaker has a superficial awareness of the subject matter;** some ideas are relevant; there is some analysis of the subject matter; some awareness of language and style is shown; ideas are occasionally supported by examples and illustrations.	3-4	**Some organization is apparent;** the oral task has some structure; supporting examples and illustrations are sometimes integrated into the oral task.	3-4	**The language sometimes lacks fluency and appropriateness;** grammar and sentence construction are sometimes accurate, although errors and inconsistencies are apparent; the register and style are to some extent appropriate to the task; the range of vocabulary and idiom is limited; the exchange flows, but there are some hesitations
5-6	**The speaker has an adequate understanding of the subject matter;** ideas are generally relevant and focused; there is evidence of critical thinking; an adequate awareness of language and style is shown; ideas are generally supported by examples.	5-6	**The oral task is organized;** the structure is mostly coherent; supporting examples and illustrations are generally well integrated into the oral task.	5-6	**The language is mostly fluent and appropriate;** there is an adequate degree of accuracy in grammar and sentence construction, although some minor errors are apparent; the register and style are mostly appropriate to the task; vocabulary and idiom are mostly varied and largely appropriate to the task; the exchange generally flows freely.
7-8	**The speaker has a good understanding of the subject matter;** ideas are mostly relevant and focused; a good degree of critical thinking is shown; a good appreciation of language and style is shown; ideas are mostly supported by examples and illustrations.	7-8	**The oral task is well organized;** the structure is mostly coherent and effective; supporting examples and illustrations are mostly well integrated into the oral task.	7-8	**The language is fluent and appropriate;** there is a good degree of accuracy in grammar and sentence construction, although the oral task is not necessarily free from error; the register and style are effective and appropriate to the task; vocabulary and idiom are varied and appropriate to the task; the exchange mostly flows freely.
9-10	**The speaker has an excellent understanding of the subject matter;** ideas are relevant and focused; a high degree of critical thinking is shown; ideas are fully supported by well chosen examples and illustrations.	9-10	**The oral task is effectively organized;** the structure is coherent and effective; supporting examples and illustrations are well integrated into the oral task.	9-10	**The language is fluent and entirely appropriate;** there is a high degree of accuracy in grammar and sentence construction, although the oral task is not necessarily free from error; the register and style are consistently effective and appropriate to the task; vocabulary and idiom are varied and highly appropriate to the task; the exchange flows freely.

- **Exile – the implications**
    - People were not as mobile as they are today, they were born and died in the same city-state
    - Their city state was part of their identity
    - Italian (and Greek) rugged terrain promoted this sense of place identity
        - terrain determined the confines of city states
    - Romeo is a Veronese – may visit Mantua but will never be a Mantuan
        - In exile identity is lost
        - (As an aside, Socrates chose to be punished by death rather than be exiled)

- **Plague – the implications**
    - In Shakespeare's time bubonic plague ravaged London in particular, England generally
    - Mercutio calls a 'plague on both' houses, Capulets and Montagues alike
    - Shakespeare's only son, Hamnet, died while Shakespeare was away from home – plague?
        - Shakespeare may not have been able to return for the funeral because of quarantine.

- **Apothecaries – the pharmacists of earlier times**
    - Mixed their own medicines
    - Potions could be medicinal or magical
        - From herbal cures of the Yarrow flower for wounds
        - to fake cures of the Angelica flower for plague
        - to roses as aphrodisiacs or love potions
        - to herbal poisons like flowering Monkshood
    - Today many doctors scoff at natural or herbalist cures
        - In Shakespeare's day physicians considered apothecaries dangerous
            - People still turn to the herbalist today as they did to the apothecary during our yesterdays

Rationale for More Than One Essay Type

Certain works of literature lend themselves to a visual analysis. Usually, the works that are in this category are those that use symbolism extensively and prominently. *Romeo and Juliet* is one of these. This is a good work to focus on language with its many levels of meaning. As well, Grade 9, the grade often designated for teaching Romeo and Juliet, is a good time to introduce the fact that the language of poetry is used in genres other than poetry.

However, since not all teachers are comfortable with this type of essay, I have included a more traditional essay assignment as well.

In the past, I have assigned both essay types to advanced classes.

Romeo and Juliet: The Visual Essay

The Visual Essay is a Purpose-Focused Poster with a balance between visual and verbal expression.

This Visual Essay focuses on a Symbol: here is a list of possibilities:
- Poisonous drugs
- Lists and Letters
- Daggers and swords
- Tools: rope, crowbar…
- Pages: Mercutio's, Romeo's, Paris'
- the Bed
- other?_______________

- **Your poster needs** to identify the play, author and where the symbol is found.
- **Your poster needs a title** that connects the symbol to a theme of the play.
- Choose excerpts for each use of the chosen symbol. All together there must be no fewer than ten lines from the play on the poster.
- Present the context (Act, Scene, Lines) like this: (V, ii, 81-83) for each excerpt. Identify the characters to whom it is connected (the speaker, the audience), perhaps comment on the excerpts' poetic language (metaphor, paradox, for example).
- Paper must be poster quality; between 8.5"x11" and 11"x15", not larger.
- You must use visuals representing the **symbol.** *Remember a symbol can have a complex significance: a drug can have a good use as well as a bad*
- Identify the **setting** pictorially.
- Your Lettering must be publishable (easily read).
- Visuals must be appropriate for our school setting.
- Research? If used, be sure to cite the source at the bottom of the poster.
- Images borrowed from the internet? That is research, so cite source.
- **The final statement must be a Theme, a statement of Truth, your Conclusion about the Symbol.**

Example: *A Visual Essay on a symbol used in Cinderella from folklore might include:*

Title: **The Significance of a Lost Shoe**..or..**Shoe, Lost and Found** *in Cinderella by Charles Perrault*

Visual: *A Shoe in the center; Cinderella's home with a French style castle in the distance and a path between (the setting).*

Verbal: *The quotations would be scattered along the path.*

Final Statement: ***Sometimes something unimportant has great significance.*** *In Cinderella a lost shoe reveals* **greed** *in Princess-want-to-bes, as it* **saves** *a worthy young woman from a life of servitude, as it* **rescues** *a prince from a disastrous marriage.*

Assessment Rubric *Visual Essay - **Romeo and Juliet***

	Ideas and Content Accurate, Analytical Imaginative Essay on a Symbol		Organization + Appearance Looks like a Poster = balances writing and visuals		Voice – Word Choice Words complement the visuals		Illustration Choice Illustrations reflect and support writing		Fluency Genre specific – Formal analysis – maintains essay standards		Mechanics Genre specific, Works are Cited
1-3	Little awareness of implications of assignment. No connection between title + final statement	1-3	Almost no awareness of requirements	1-2	The person behind the writing is missing, no personality evident.	1-2	Limited or inappropriate illustrations	1-2	Language lacks fluency and/or appropriateness	1-2	Incomprehensible due to errors of grammar, punctuation, spelling
4-6	Superficial / obvious connection between title final statement	4-6	Limited awareness of requirements of this poster	3-4	A voice is beginning to emerge but a bland version	3-4	Uninteresting, bland and limited Vision.	3-4	Limited variation in expression which creates rigidity.	3-4	Mechanical errors abound + interfere with comprehension
7-9	Some originality, Reflects some varied connections	7-9	Some awareness of requirements.	5-7	The reader has some sense of the person behind the writing, somewhat interesting	5-7	Some interesting visuals but repetitious or disconnected	5-7	Some fluency but errors, or bland language, interfere with message; dull.	5-7	Fewer mechanical errors, but they affect the reading of text
10-12	More original, meets essay requirements. Reflects good analysis and makes literal connections	10-12	Adequate control of basic requirements	8-10	You are more engaged with your writing, though the writing is predictable	8-10	Illustrations are appropriate, but predictable.	8-10	More fluent with the beginning of a sense of style.	8-10	Mechanical errors persist with some impact on communication + comprehension
13-15	Mostly original ideas; meets visual essay requirements. Some connections reflect abstract thought	13-15	Mostly meets essay/ assignment requirements	11-12	You are engaged with your writing, almost exciting.	11-12	Good illustration choices, good connections, almost exciting	11-12	Fluent with a clearer sense of style, balancing language of the essay with limitations of a poster	11-12	Evidence of serious editing, errors have little impact on comprehension
16-18	Original, creative – almost publishable – shows **balanced** use of the concrete and the abstract	16-18	Well **balanced**, meets essay requirements	13-14	Good evidence of a personality; the writer is clearly heard – varied vocabulary	13-14	Effective + varied illustrations; connects to purpose	13-14	The writing is fluent, easy to understand and shows style. Almost memorable	13-14	Clean. Obvious evidence of editing.
19-20	Highly original, creative; publishable exciting	19-20	Essay requirements are met naturally and smoothly	15	A lively and distinct voice reflecting your unique personality.	15	Rich, colorful, precise, effective; grips audience	15	The writing has rhythm + power. Language is exciting + varied	15	Polished. Almost technically perfect.

Romeo and Juliet: Analytical Essay – Due in two weeks

- Be formal (Hook at the beginning of the Introduction; Thesis Statement at the end of the Introduction; Body paragraphs following the order of points presented in the Thesis Statement; Impact Statement at the end of the Conclusion; Impersonally analytical with no unsupported opinion, therefore do not use first-person pronouns)
- Minimum of 700 words
- Place the word count at the end of the essay in a Works Cited page.
- Cite sources using MLA style – the Works Cited page is not part of your word count.
- Incorporate minimum of two citations directly from the play. These must not be more than 20% of your word count. More than 20% is considered plagiarism.

State your choice of topic within two days.

Choice One – The Foils! *Research* may be useful but is not necessary.
- Define 'foil' as it is used in literature. (Introduction)
- Choose an important character who is partially described, through contrast, by a foil.
  - What characteristics (physical? personality? social?) are emphasized through the contrast?
  - Is the foil important in his/her own right?

Choice Two – Who Inherits? This option requires *Research*
- Describe the laws of Inheritance for Elizabethan England (Introduction)
- The Montagues lost Romeo, their only child.
  - Who inherits their estate? Their social position?
- The Capulets lost Juliet, their only child.
  - Who inherits their estate? Their social position?
- Speculate: According to your research, what viable options are available?
- In Act 5 everyone in Verona learns that Romeo and Juliet were married; does this affect who inherits?

Choice Three – To what degree is Friar Lawrence responsible for the fate of Romeo and Juliet? - *Research* may be useful but is not necessary
- Describe the role of the friar confessor/mentor (Introduction)
- Way(s) he bears *Total Responsibility* = he should have known the outcome
- Way(s) he bears *Partial Responsibility* = he should have been able to anticipate the outcome as one of a few possibilities
- Way(s) he bears *Minimal Responsibility* = while he could not have anticipated the outcome, he could have reacted more quickly and effectively
- He bears No Responsibility = he could not have anticipated what happened.

Romeo & Juliet—Analytical Essay Rubric

Ideas and Content + thesis, conclusion + citing		Organization		Voice		Word Choice		Sentence Fluency		Mechanics – MLA formatting	
1-3	Little awareness of implications of the question.	1-3	Little organization, structure.	1-2	The person behind the writing is missing, no personality evident.	1-2	Limited +/or inappropriate language for audience	1-2	Language lacks fluency and appropriateness	1-2	Incomprehensible due to errors of grammar, punctuation, spelling
4-6	Ideas are superficial and not supported.	4-6	Some organization but little integration of supporting data.	3-4	A voice is beginning to emerge.	3-4	Uninteresting, bland vocabulary limited awareness of audience	3-4	Limited variation in sentence structure which creates rigidity.	3-4	Mechanical errors abound + interfere with comprehension
7-9	Some analysis, some support, little critical thinking.	7-9	Some organization, some integration of supporting data.	5-7	The reader has some sense of the person behind the writing.	5-7	Some interesting vocabulary but repetitious, some awareness of audience	5-7	Some fluency but sentence structure errors interfere with comprehension.	5-7	Fewer mechanical errors, but they affect the reading of text
10-12	Adequate analysis/ideas, adequate support, some critical thinking.	10-12	Adequate organization with adequate integration of supporting data	8-10	You are more engaged with your writing, the writer sometimes comes through.	8-10	Word choice is appropriate, but predictable. More aware of audience	8-10	More fluent with the beginning of a sense of style. Limited sentence variety.	8-10	Mechanical errors persist with some impact on communication + comprehension
13-15	Mostly relevant ideas, mostly well supported.	13-15	Good organization with good integration of supporting data	11-12	You are engaged with your writing, though it is generic at times.	11-12	Good word choice, good connections, almost exciting	11-12	Fluent with a clearer sense of style and more varied sentences	11-12	Evidence of serious editing, errors have little impact on comprehension
16-18	Relevant and focused ideas; good support + critical thinking	16-18	Well balanced organization with effective integration of data	13-14	Good evidence of a personality ; the writer is clearly heard.	13-14	Effective + varied vocabulary, connects to audience/ purpose	13-14	The writing is fluent, easy to understand and shows style. Almost memorable	13-14	Clean. Obvious evidence of editing.
19-20	Highly relevant, well supported ideas; excellent critical thinking	19-20	Well organized and persuasive; coherent structure,integrated data.	15	A lively and distinct voice with a unique personality	15	Rich, colorful, precise, effective; enhances purpose, grips audience	15	The writing has rhythm + power. Sentences are consistently varied in length + structure	15	Polished. Almost technically perfect. Carefully and thoroughly edited.

About Mary Richards

Being the daughter of an Anglican missionary priest sent to a remote area of a developing country, my six siblings and I certainly did not live in luxury. This could have led to a poverty perspective on life; it did not because in our home there was a wealth of books and music. While too often there was barely enough money for enough food, there was always money for another record for my mother and a new volume for my father. The worlds created by the great artists of the distant past and innovative authors of the near past were where I often lived. Romeo and Juliet's Verona was one such alternative reality.

Teaching became a consuming passion centered on this love of literature. In time I learned to transfer my mothering-love of younger siblings to students. With a Permanent Teaching Certificate from the United States, renewed and reworked in Canada, I have taught at every grade level from Nursery to University. My M. Ed. has an International Education focus. With IB and AP certifications, I have taught in Panama, El Salvador, Mexico, Zambia, as well as in Canada. I have worked in the smallest of private schools as well as in a large public provincial university. Everywhere I have been has had the required literature and basic materials, but also has had gaps that needed to be filled.

These Teaching Tools are the materials I created to fill these gaps. I wanted to put the literature into historical and cultural context, hence the lecture notes. I wanted the students to appreciate the language chosen by the author, which requires close reading and closer listening, hence the quizzes and oral presentation. I wanted the students to think about what they had read as deeply as possible and to express these thoughts in writing, hence the various essay prompts. I have tweaked and refined these over my 40+ year career. As retirement begins, my current purpose is to get as many of these Teaching Tools out there as possible. This *Romeo and Juliet* Teaching Tool is the third in a growing series.

9 798470 748102